Loitering Laws

Loitering Laws

Jim Crow Lingers in Modern Times

CALVIN HIGHT ALLEN

Faraway publishing
Black Mountain, N.C.

Copyright © 2025 by Calvin Hight Allen
All rights reserved. First Edition

The author may be contacted at
Wayside E-35, Givens Highland Farms, 200 Tabernacle Road
Black Mountain, NC 28711
calvinwnc@gmail.com

Published by
FARAWAY PUBLISHING
125 Spring View Drive
Black Mountain, N.C. 28711
farawaypublishing@gmail.com

Faraway Publishing respects copyright protection, which is essential for creativity, diverse storytelling, and free speech. Thank you for procuring an authorized edition of this book and for honoring copyright laws by not reproducing, scanning, or distributing any part of it in any form without permission from the author. Your support helps our authors and enables Faraway Publishing to continue publishing books for all readers.

ISBN: 979-8-9990731-0-5 (pbk.)
Library of Congress Control Number: 2025939739

Printed in the United States of America
10 9 8 7 6 5 4 3 2 1

Cover Photo "Folks Watching Juggler on Wall Street" by Calvin Allen
All photos by Calvin Allen unless otherwise captioned

Dedication

For Fred Shuttlesworth and civil rights activists

All who wander are not lost.

    J.R.R. Tolkien

However, they can be questioned without cause.

    Loitering Laws

Contents

Dedication	v
Introduction	x
Foreword	xi
Prologue	xii
Section 1: History of Loitering Laws	**1**
Jim Crow Outlaws Loitering	3
Vagrancy—a Synonym of Loitering.	4
Salvadoran Man Questioned for Loitering	5
Old Traditions Die Slowly	7
The Medium Is the Message?	10
Section 2: Loitering While Unusual/Suspicious	**11**
Five Jokes for a Dollar	12
Who Would Park under a No Loitering Sign?	13
Tiger Trolls for Trouble	14
Is Crawling with a Cat Criminal?	15
Does Juggler Cause This Crowd to Loiter?	16
Is Strolling While Rolling Suspicious?	17
Troubled Soul Creeps in Pritchard Park	18
Is It Unlawful for a Burly Person to Sport Daisy Dukes?	19
Watch Your Body Language!	20
Old Men Tarrying by a Truck	21
Tableau of Tarrying	22
Creeping with a Carryall	23
Scruffy Scofflaw Lurks at Library	24
Is His Hinus Loitering?	25
Purple Plodder Procrastinates on Patton	26
Trio of Tarry-ers Target Jewels?	27
Two Gentlemen Discuss Asheville's Panhandling Laws	28
Synchronicity Causes the Writer to Go Off Subject	29
Woolworth Wait?	30
Section 3: Loitering Is in the Eye of the Law	**31**
I'm a Soul Man 👱	32

Are Police Allowed to Loiter?..33
Tourists Loitering with Impunity...34
Folks Tarrying around a Table..35
Little Red Riding Hood Strolls by the Wolfpack.................................36
Why Am I Tarrying with These Two?..37
Does Personal Appearance Affect the Story?....................................38
How Does a Motorist Become a Loiterer?..39
Andre Michaux Looms Over Loiterer 40
Large Urban Backpacks Scream "Loiterer".. 41
Trio Tarries on Broadway 42
Waiting Woman Flirts with Loitering 43
Loitering for Their Buses 44
When Does Lolling Become Loitering?..45
See Spot Loiter..46
If You Saunter Slowly, Are You Loitering?..47
Are Tourists Allowed to Loiter?...48
Lounging in Pritchard Park...49
Playing for Procrastinators 50
Creeping on the Corner... 51
Pokey Peddler Pauses in Pritchard Park 52
What Did the Buddhist Say to the Hotdog Vendor?........................53
How Much Decelerating is Too Much?..54
NEVER Single Out a Photographer..55
Dilly Dalliers Dodge the Law with Ruse..56
Photography Makes Loiterers Out of Pedestrians...........................57
Do Tourists Loiter Legally?...58
Dapper Dawdlers Are Free to Dilly Dally..59
Why Are You Hiding Under That Hoodie, Sir? 60
Folks Have Puttered at Pack Square since 1903............................... 61
All the Warning Signs are Here...62
If the Truck is Not Idling, Is the Driver? 63
The Nurse and the Noodler 64
What Do You See?..65

    Filibustering at the Federal Building 66
    Lord, I Was Born a Ramblin Man...67
    What Is This Waiting Woman Eyeballing? 68
    Six Loiterers Make a Story 69
    Tap, Tap, Tap, . . . Tarry? 70
    Don't Just Sit There, DO Something! 71
    Sir, Let Me See Your Loitering Card 72
Section 4: Loitering While Unhoused 73
    Snug Harbor 74
    Take a Number—Then Move Along 75
    The Cycle of Life 76
    Pair of Procrastinators Perched at Pritchard Park......................................77
    Poking Along by the Parking Deck 78
Section 5: Loitering While of Color 79
    TWE (Texting While Ethnic) 80
    A Sojourner of a Different Stripe 81
    When Does Lingering Become Malingering? 82
    Your Move, Officer 83
    Don't Skulk on the Steps 84
    Walking While Black..85
Epilogue 86

Introduction

Twenty-nine-year-old Salvadoran Kilmar Armando Abrego Garcia is imprisoned in a notorious high-security prison in El Salvador. Although he has never been convicted of a crime, he was detained and questioned for loitering, a centuries-old law, ruled unconstitutional, and yet still haunting folks who linger in public.

Loitering.

Although the signs for Whites Only drinking fountains and restrooms are gone, loitering signs remain—a reminder that United States citizens live in a society of classes. Folks in the lower classes who travel in public are at the mercy of law enforcement—just for standing out or, as one civil rights activist alleges, just for being.

Foreword

Mr. Allen's observations of the different species of loiterers and near-loiterers were a real eye-opener for me. However, I wish he had included some drawings of some of these species after being dissected. What does the INSIDE of a loiterer look like?

—Audrey Plantagenet, great-great-great-great niece of André Michaux

Prologue

"A Moral Duty to Act"

Sometimes minding your own business is not good enough—especially if you're doing it in public. Kilmar Abrego Garcia was hanging out with friends in a parking lot; now he's imprisoned in a maximum-security prison in El Salvador. Fred Shuttlesworth was walking on the sidewalk in Birmingham, AL; he was questioned and then arrested by a police officer, stayed in jail for months, and was released only after The Supreme Court ruled unanimously that Birmingham's loitering law was unconstitutional. More than half of those in <u>U.S. Immigration and Customs Enforcement</u> detention facilities have no criminal record, according to an April NBC analysis.

All these arrests have things in common—the people who were questioned and then arrested stood out: black or brown skin, tattoos or distinctive clothing, and they were in public.

As you travel in public places, remember your duty to stand up for the underclass. "The price of privilege is the moral duty to act when one sees another person treated unfairly. And the least that a person in the dominant caste can do is not make the pain any worse."

—Isabel Wilkerson, <u>Caste: The Origins of Our Discontents</u>

Section 1: History of Loitering Laws

Although Unconstitutional, Loitering Laws Linger.

Loitering. Vagrancy. Skulking. Prowling. Slinking. Idling.

When you are waiting in a public place, do you ever feel awkward? That you should keep busy? That hanging around might get you in trouble? If a "No Loitering" sign is nearby, do those feelings intensify?

America's laws against lingering have roots in Medieval and Elizabethan England, according to *Wikipedia*. Since 1342, the goal has always been to keep anyone "out of place" away, according to Ariel Aberg-Riger of the Equal Justice Initiative (https://eji.org/about/), a non-profit that fights mass incarceration and excessive punishment. Since the 14th Century, laws against loitering have allowed police to question, harass, and arrest people who loiter. The first law was passed after the Black Death plague decimated the English population and lords were concerned that there might not be enough workers to harvest crops. Workers, realizing they were in high demand, might refuse to work for unsuitable pay, and this caused friction between them and their overlords.

Is holding out for better pay loitering? The definition and enforcement of loitering has been contentious ever since. On one side, shopkeepers and other business owners say society needs loitering laws to prevent scruffy folks from blocking shop doors, panhandling, and camping—activities that discourage customers. On the other side, civil rights activists say loitering laws allow police too much leeway to target youth, the poor, and people of color. "When it comes down to it, loitering is just being," writes Aberg-Riger.

Jim Crow Outlaws Loitering

After President Abraham Lincoln was assassinated on April 14, 1865, new President Andrew Johnson offered blanket amnesty to all former Confederates who swore a loyalty oath, and Johnson pardoned hundreds more, according to the book *Democracy Awakening*, by Heather Cox Richardson. Thus, former Confederates were free to write Jim Crow laws, returning freedmen to near-slavery. One of the new laws required freedmen to sign yearlong work contracts every January—or be judged vagrants and fined or imprisoned, according to Richardson.

Vagrancy—a Synonym of Loitering.

In another famous loitering case, civil rights activist Fred Shuttlesworth was arrested in 1962 for "obstructing free passage on the sidewalk and for refusing to obey a police officer," according to the website of *Oyez*, a multimedia archive of the Supreme Court of the United States. Shuttlesworth was found guilty in Birmingham, AL city court and appealed all the way to the US Supreme Court, which unanimously found that the law was unconstitutional. Shuttlesworth spearheaded the Civil Rights movement in Birmingham and was beaten, bombed, and fire-hosed for his efforts. Read more about Shuttlesworth at https://www.al.com/opinion/2022/03/guest-opinion-the-civil-rights-leader-nobody-knows-on-his-100th-birthday.html, an opinion piece in AL.com, an internet site about Alabama.

Salvadoran Man Questioned for Loitering

Kilmar Abrego Garcia. Photo by Associated Press.

"On 03/28/2019 at approximately 1427 hours, Detective ▇ with the Hyattsville City Police observed four individuals loitering in the parking lot of the Home Depot located at 3301 East-West Highway in Hyattsville, MD 20782," read the Prince George's County Police Department Gang Field Interview Sheet. One of those individuals was Kilmar Abrego Garcia, the Salvadoran at the center of a firestorm over constitutional rights. No person shall "be deprived of life, liberty, or property, without due process of law," according to the Fifth Amendment of the United States Constitution. After the Trump administration deported (without due process) Abrego Garcia to a prison in El Salvador, the US Court of Appeals for Fourth Circuit ruled that Abrego Garcia be returned to the United States. The US Supreme Court agreed, ruling that the Trump administration "facilitate" his return. However, Abrego Garcia remains in the Salvadoran prison.

Old Traditions Die Slowly

In 1901, Richard Sharpe Smith, who had designed the Vance Memorial at Pack Square five years earlier, was commissioned by the

Asheville Club, a social male-only club, to build an impressive new building, where the club's wealthy and influential members could convene, according to Lavilo.com.

Herbert Delahaye Miles, who had moved to Asheville in 1913 to seek a cure for his wife's tuberculosis, bought the building in 1919. By 1925 he had remodeled the exterior and had converted the interior into office space. He then renamed the building to *Miles Building*.

Today, the Miles Building downtown sports an antiquated sign concerning loiterers.

Sometimes "loitering" behaviors are clearly undesirable, such as when drunk folks pass out in front of a shop. However, say civil-rights proponents, society doesn't need loitering laws because public drunkenness and urban camping are already illegal.

Police liked loitering laws, alleges Aberg-Riger, because the laws were vague and thus allowed police to question—and arrest—almost anyone in public. "That included homeless veterans returning from the war, single women on street corners, vendors peddling goods, dissidents peddling thoughts, the mentally ill, poor, queer, or Black people," he wrote.

Even today, in Florida, "[i]t is unlawful for any person to loiter or prowl in a place, at a time or in a manner not usual for law-abiding individuals, under circumstances that warrant a justifiable and reasonable alarm or immediate concern for the safety of persons or property in the vicinity," according to a Cornell Law School website.

As you look at the photographs in this book, ask yourself whether the people photographed are loitering, gathering, skulking, recruiting, celebrating, prowling, talking, sneaking, dancing, or just being themselves. If you were a police officer, which groups would you address? What does your decision say about your job? About you? About our culture?

Move it along—nothing to see here.

The Medium Is the Message?

Just as foliage has obscured this No Loitering sign, loitering laws de jure are fading from the books—but they are still enforced de facto.

Section 2: Loitering While Unusual/Suspicious

Five Jokes for a Dollar

Backlit by the setting sun, a man sits on the sidewalk, his baseball cap holding a few bills and some change. He offers to sell me "five jokes for a dollar." He's breaking at least one Asheville law by panhandling in "a high-traffic area." Neither the city nor the state of North Carolina prohibit loitering per se. Additional offenses, such as blocking traffic, must occur. However, state law states: "Any police officer may arrest any person suspected of being a loiterer or prowler without a warrant if it reasonably appears that the delay in arresting the suspect caused by obtaining a warrant would result in the suspect's escape." Escape from what? Suspicion?

Who Would Park under a No Loitering Sign?

Photo by Jim White

Why would anyone procrastinate under a NO LOITERING sign—unless they were a scofflaw? Jim White was lucky he didn't feel the hand of the law tapping his shoulder while he was taking this shot.

Tiger Trolls for Trouble

A man wearing a Clemson Tigers backpack and dragging a torn garbage bag rummages in a nook on College St. He's not idle, blocking the sidewalk, panhandling, camping in public, or raving. However, I'll bet you a bitcoin that he'd be questioned for loitering.

Is Crawling with a Cat Criminal?

A barefoot pilgrim stands on a corner in downtown Asheville, a cat draped over his shoulders. Although the city has no loitering laws (or no No Loitering laws?), the pilgrim is supposed to have his feline on a leash, according to Section 3-27 of the city code.

Does Juggler Cause This Crowd to Loiter?

According to a strict interpretation of Asheville law, these folks watching a juggler perform are loitering—they are blocking the sidewalk in a high-traffic area. If you were a police officer, would you ask them to disperse? Ask to see the performer's permit? Enjoy the show?

Is Strolling While Rolling Suspicious?

Although Asheville is a tourist town, the city's residents rarely see folks rolling their carry-ons downtown. This man might have a perfectly good reason for rolling luggage, but in other towns with No-Loitering laws the police might have probable cause to stop and unpack those reasons.

Troubled Soul Creeps in Pritchard Park

This fellow seemed to be having a rough morning. After sitting up and screaming for a few minutes, he pulled his bag around him and lay down. Although Asheville does not have loitering laws, it is illegal to disturb the peace or camp in public.

Is It Unlawful for a Burly Person to Sport Daisy Dukes?

They're not loitering, because they're walking. However, are those Daisy Dukes? Shaved legs? Let's run this laggard in . . . or at least question them.

Watch Your Body Language!

These old guys might have gotten away with idling on the corner if the codger in the red cap hadn't hunched over like a skulker. As it played out, they were taken to the pokey and charged with escaping a secure facility.

Old Men Tarrying by a Truck

Everything about this scene is suspicious: why do the old men look so RED? Why are they hanging around in a noisy, smelly parking deck? Why is that truck so shiny? What are they talking about that they can't discuss while walking?

Tableau of Tarrying

At the central bus station, a man stands, backed up against a fence, his head dropped. In the background, another man talks on the phone while standing in the middle of a parking lot. A "No Trespassing" sign is attached to the fence. If you're a security officer, do you speak to either of them?

Creeping with a Carryall

Spotted in Black Mountain, this person was rolling their carryall on a little wheeled contraption. They slung it ahead of them on the sidewalk, caught it with their foot when it rolled back down the hill, and then slung it forward again. Although a quick search of the city's municipal codes turned up no laws against loitering, officers could stop this person from blocking the sidewalk or cite them for whiplashing a carryall.

Scruffy Scofflaw Lurks at Library

Although he is not completely blocking the sidewalk, this old man's ragged appearance and provocative ponytail beg law enforcement to question this skulker.

Is His Hinus Loitering?

The person sitting on the wall is getting dangerously close to violating state law regarding indecent exposure, according to FindLaw.com. Folks are not allowed to display their "private parts" in a public place, including genitals, pubic area, nipples, and anus. No mention of gluteal folds.

Purple Plodder Procrastinates on Patton

Sitting shoeless on the sidewalk in front of a bank on Patton Avenue, this person doesn't have a leg to stand on, legally or literally. They are blocking the sidewalk, disturbing the peace (they were lecturing passersby loudly), and maybe displaying public drunkenness.

Trio of Tarry-ers Target Jewels?

Two men and a woman talk in the parking lot of Spicer Greene Jewelers, while a car door stands open behind them.

Could they be talking about a smash-and-grab robbery of the store? What's in the backpacks? The trunk of the car? If you were a store security guard, would you call the police? How would you describe the scene?

Two Gentlemen Discuss Asheville's Panhandling Laws

Tall: "Have you read the city's new laws regarding panhandling?"

Rainbow: "Yeah. I love the heading 'Creating a safe environment for caring,' followed by a list of no-nos."

Tall (laughs): "They could have saved a lot of time with just the one rule: 'No panhandling in high-traffic zones.' Where the hell else would we panhandle?"

Rainbow: "At least they don't call it 'loitering' any more. Hate that word!"

Synchronicity Causes the Writer to Go Off Subject

While I was researching NC law regarding unicycles and loitering, I came across this nugget from the general statutes: "It's important to note that operating a unicycle while under the influence of alcohol or drugs can lead to a DWI charge, as any type of vehicle, including a unicycle, canoe, or car can be the basis for a DWI charge." A canoe? I can see it now: a canoeist pulled over by a warden. Officer: "Let's see you paddle a straight line." Paddler: "But officer, I never learned the J stroke." Or two inmates at the county jail: "What you in for?" "Paddling under the influence."

Woolworth Wait?

A person with a backpack and large plastic bag sits in front of Woolworth Walk downtown.

Are they loitering or just sitting? Does it matter that they gyrate their torso frantically from time to time? What if Woolworths was open? If you were the manager, would you call the police?

Section 3: Loitering Is in the Eye of the Law

Now that loitering laws are mostly gone from city codes, it is left to the intuition of public safety officers to decide who to question.

I'm a Soul Man 👶

The Jehovah's Witnesses regularly set up on this corner at Pritchard Park. Are they loitering? While the city has no laws specifically outlawing proselytizing, ordinances do prohibit "verbal panhandling" in high-traffic areas.

Are Police Allowed to Loiter?

Two men sit on a wall and talk in Pritchard Park, a public park in downtown Asheville. Are they loitering? Would your answer change if you knew that one or both of the men are police officers?

Tourists Loitering with Impunity

Four adults, one carrying a child, stand on a corner outside the Grove Arcade. Will the police bother them for tarrying? How does the type and condition of a backpack affect your perception? The child? Their appearance? The color of their skin?

Folks Tarrying around a Table

Five or six people tarry around a table in Pritchard Park. You're a police officer patrolling the park. Do you question them? What if a cannabis flag hangs from the table? What if the table is blocking the steps?

Little Red Riding Hood Strolls by the Wolfpack

Hey there Little Red Riding Hood,

You sure are lookin' good,

You're everything that a big bad wolf could want.

OOOOOOOOOOWWWWWWWWW!

Can you think of a tale featuring loitering? Did the hare loiter while the tortoise steadily walked? Did the Tar Baby loiter in the path, waiting for Brer Rabbit?

Why Am I Tarrying with These Two?

The guy in the black shirt might be having an epiphany. While the other two discuss the gang's next caper, our epiphanized hombre hangs his head and ponders: do I have morons on my team? Do I want to be locked in a cell with these two twerps? Are we loitering?

Does Personal Appearance Affect the Story?

Legally, the nicely dressed couple are loitering by blocking the entrance to the market. Legally, the Man in Black with the extreme mullet, dancing to his phone, is not loitering. If you owned the market, which of these folks would you want to chase off?

How Does a Motorist Become a Loiterer?

A heavy-footed hitchhiker is dropped off at a rest area. While trying to catch their next ride, they are accosted by security for loitering.

"Hey, buddy, move it along."

"But officer, I can't walk on the highway!"

"Not my problem. Vamoose! Or your next ride will be to the pokey."

Andre Michaux Looms Over Loiterer

The ghost of André Michaux watches in amazement as a woman enjoys a cigarette outside the Dripolator. Haunted by the death of his young wife and propelled through life by the fervent urge to discover new plants, renowned botanist Michaux traveled the world (including Black Mountain), never once taking time to loiter.

Large Urban Backpacks Scream "Loiterer"

Although he could argue that he's a customer enjoying a take-out meal al fresco, this man's backpack might trigger a police officer to ask him a few questions.

Trio Tarries on Broadway

A man watches a toddler toddle down Broadway, while a seated man with a drink scratches his leg.

Can a man loiter while watching a child? What if it's a scruffy man watching kids on a public playground?

Is the other man loitering? What if he had no drink and had laid his head on the table?

Waiting Woman Flirts with Loitering

A woman studies something in her hand while standing in the middle of the sidewalk on Broadway.

What is she looking at? Is it any of the police's business? Is she blocking the sidewalk? Waiting to cross the street? Why stop in front of a closed jewelry store? If you were a police officer, you'd have the power to ask her.

Loitering for Their Buses

Folks wait at the main Asheville Redefines Transit Station.

If you wanted to loiter, this is a place where you might get away with it. Should security ask them their destination? What if they are sleeping on a bench? Staggering in a bus lane? Toting an AR-17?

When Does Lolling Become Loitering?

Five women in purple pants loll at the bottom of some stairs in front of the Battery Park Hotel, while another person sits on a bench.

Because they are partially blocking the steps, does a police officer have the right to search the five's bags? What if they were Black young men? Black young men sitting on the steps?

See Spot Loiter

Can a person be interrogated while walking their dog? What if you were rest-stop security and saw a scruffy person wearing a backpack and leading a dog on a rope?

If You Saunter Slowly, Are You Loitering?

A woman carrying two backpacks saunters on the sidewalk of Patton Avenue downtown.

What's in her backpacks? Where is she going? Why is she downtown? If you were a police officer, you could ask her.

Are Tourists Allowed to Loiter?

A pair of couples and four walkers occupy Pritchard Park in Asheville, a tourist town. Where is the line drawn between resting tourists and loitering scalawags? How does the water bottle carried by one walker affect your perception? The purple hair? The bag from a downtown shop in the boy's lap?

Lounging in Pritchard Park

Two men with backpacks sit and study their phones on a bench in Pritchard Park. Are they loitering? If you were a strolling tourist, would their presence make you nervous? Would they affect which sidewalk you might choose to walk on? What if they were talking loudly? If they were playing chess?

Playing for Procrastinators

A busker plays a stringed instrument while walkers pass and folks sit across from him. Is the busker exempt from loitering laws because of his instrument? Does he need to be playing to be exempt? How well? Are the folks sitting on the wall listeners or lollygaggers? What if they are scruffy?

Creeping on the Corner

On one hand, these three could be checking their phones. Waiting to use the new, fresh-air-ventilated, all-gender public toilet. On the other hand, to a jaundiced eye, they could be loitering until their partners-in-crime signal them to storm Tops for Shoes. Your call.

Pokey Peddler Pauses in Pritchard Park

Pritchard Park is a gathering place for tourists, buskers, downtown workers, homeless folk, street preachers, and performers. Which category do these two belong in? Are they in the same category?

What Did the Buddhist Say to the Hotdog Vendor?

At first glance, it appears that a customer is waiting under a "No Loitering" sign for his dog. Does the sign mean that he can't eat the dog at the stand? That he needs to move along after he finishes? Or has the stand had trouble with No-Good-Niks skulking near the window, sniffing free dog fumes?

The Buddhist said, "Make me one with everything."

How Much Decelerating is Too Much?

Sitting in the driver's seat, this person seems to be reading the label on a can. If you're in the public safety industry, do you check the parking meter to make sure it's paid up? Do you consider the air freshener to be drug paraphernalia?

NEVER Single Out a Photographer

A man alerts a woman to the presence of a photographer who's snapping their photo. According to The Street Photographer's Manual, "any person pointing to or otherwise calling attention to a photographer in a public place is automatically considered to be loitering, and may be subject to a citizen's arrest by said photographer."

Dilly Dalliers Dodge the Law with Ruse

One of the oldest tricks that loiterers use to avoid hassle from the police is to hug as though they know each other. The big smile really sells it, but a shrewd officer can see right through.

Photography Makes Loiterers Out of Pedestrians

In this photo, walkers using a downtown crosswalk are frozen into loitering. When I presented the photo to a police officer, he said,

"Were they walking when you took the shot?"

"Does it look like they're walking?" I replied.

He glanced at the photo again. "Yes, it does," he said.

"But they're not moving," I protested.

He looked at me, clearly annoyed. "YOU better get moving, or I'll arrest you for annoying an officer."

Do Tourists Loiter Legally?

They are standing around on the sidewalk. She's wearing a backpack. If they were in a city with No Loitering laws, would they be questioned? Why not?

Dapper Dawdlers Are Free to Dilly Dally

If civil rights activists are correct and police decide who to question/arrest based on appearance, these Dilly-Dalliers are probably safe, even though they are idle.

Why Are You Hiding Under That Hoodie, Sir?

Have hoodies gone mainstream? They used to be a Black thing, I think, but now everybody's getting in on the action. This guy is sporting one: maybe he's self-conscious about his bald spot; maybe the breeze is cool; maybe he's trying to blend in at Pritchard Park. Whatever the reason, he may be in for a rude awakening, according to a quick internet search—some police still regard hoodies as suspicious clothing.

Folks Have Puttered at Pack Square since 1903

A bearded young man with a backpack and a reusable mug sits in front of the Biltmore Building at Pack Square. He's not dressed for a job interview, and he's idle. Should the police move him along? He's not blocking the door, but Biltmore clients might have something to say about his appearance. However, Pack Square was created as a public space in 1903, according to *Wikipedia*. It includes the Biltmore Building.

All the Warning Signs are Here

At first glance, this man is reading his phone while taking a break. But Barney Fife and other hypervigilant officers would point out the warning signs: he's left the door open for a quick escape; he's carrying hollow pipes, perfect for concealing contraband; he's refusing to make eye contact with the photographer; and he's got his cap brim low to avoid CCTV cameras.

If the Truck is Not Idling, Is the Driver?

How long may you sit in your parked car before attracting attention from the police? Loitering includes, "Remaining idle in one location, including walking around aimlessly and sitting or standing in or out of a motor vehicle," according to the American Legal Publishing website. Smoking a cigarette on a Tuesday morning, this man is waiting/taking a break/idling in his truck in a metered spot. Asheville's downtown meters are enforced Monday through Saturday from 8 am until 6 pm, so he's probably ok if he's fed the meter. What if he was sitting on the tailgate? Leaning against the hood? Lying down in the front seat?

The Nurse and the Noodler

In the foreground, a woman in scrubs walks on a sidewalk. In the background, a woman sits smoking on a low tree planter. Is either loitering? What if the background woman had no cigarette? Was sitting by a bus stop? What if the foreground woman were dressed in rags and pushing a shopping cart?

What Do You See?

    This tableau is a Rorschach test for observers. Do you see two folks waiting for Tupelo Honey to open? A Black man trying to panhandle a white woman? A cautious woman keeping her distance from the scary Black gangsta? A photojournalist with too much time on his hands?

Filibustering at the Federal Building

A person sits cross-legged on a column in front of the Veach-Baley Federal Complex. They aren't blocking traffic, panhandling, or protesting. Are they loitering? There are no federal loitering laws but, ironically, very strict loitering laws for criminals inside federal prisons. If you were a federal marshal parking in front of this person, would you question them?

Lord, I Was Born a Ramblin Man

A man with a backpack leans on a bollard in front of the Veach-Baley Federal Complex in downtown Asheville. If you're in charge of security at the complex, what do you do about him?

What Is This Waiting Woman Eyeballing?

A woman is sitting on a bench at Pritchard Park. Is she loitering? On the one hand, she is white and well-dressed. On the other hand, she is wearing dark glasses. Is she casing the store across the street for a gang of scalawags? If she had a grocery buggy full of stuff parked beside her, would the police question her? If you were a police officer, would you chat her up? Ask to see ID? What if she were a young skateboarder? Carrying full garbage bags?

Six Loiterers Make a Story

Maybe the man behind the lectern is chastising the white-haired man for blocking the hotel's front door. The white-haired man is perhaps a hotel guest who was planning to ask directions from the bellhop until the chastising. The man on the left is ogling the two women, who are innocent bywalkers. The reflection might be a photographer in search of loiterers.

Tap, Tap, Tap, . . . Tarry?

A person with a white cane smokes downtown. What are they doing besides smoking? Are we allowed to take our time in public? Do idle hands do the devil's work?

Don't Just Sit There, DO Something!

Three people sit in Pritchard Park. Two of them appear to be holding phones, while the other is idle. How does idleness affect your view of a person?

Sir, Let Me See Your Loitering Card

A man with a big plastic bag and a backpack stands at the entrance to Pack Library. He leans against the brick wall, waiting (perhaps for 10 o'clock, when the library opens)? Is he loitering? If you were a police officer, would you talk with him? What if he were Black? Sitting down? Lying on the bricks? Talking to himself?

Section 4: Loitering While Unhoused

Snug Harbor

Because of road construction, Woodfin Place, which runs from Broadway up to Flint, was blocked on both ends, and motorists couldn't drive to the parking lot in this photo. A person has built a camp in the southeast corner of the lot. They are sheltered by a tall concrete wall on one side, and they have added a wooden pallet and a shopping cart to enclose their domain. They aren't blocking anything. If you were a tourist, how would you react to this scene? (Camping is illegal in downtown Asheville.) Should the police clear them out?

Take a Number—Then Move Along

This sign in the parking lot of the Buncombe County Department of Health and Human Services prohibits loitering.

The Cycle of Life

When I spoke with this pilgrim, who carries all his possessions on his bicycle, he told me that the police don't bother him.

"I don't rant and rave like the meth-heads," he said, sipping from a jigger of bourbon in Pritchard Park. "I don't block any entrances or [defecate] in doorways. I like to think of myself as local color."

Pair of Procrastinators Perched at Pritchard Park

A woman and man linger on a bench at Pritchard Park. Her big belly swathed in red, she's frowning. Wrapped in a sleeping bag/poncho/blanket, he's holding a cigar. Are they loitering? If you're a social worker, what story do you tell about them? If you're a police officer? A tourist?

Poking Along by the Parking Deck

Wearing a backpack and a leather cap and carrying a red stuff-sack, a person walks down Walnut Street. Are they loitering? What if they were wearing a suit and carrying a briefcase?

Section 5: Loitering While of Color

TWE (Texting While Ethnic)

Imagine you're a white police officer, born and raised in western North Carolina. You joined the force mainly for the car chases. After you totaled three cruisers, the brass transferred you to the downtown beat. Which trio looks suspicious?

A Sojourner of a Different Stripe

A person with a backpack and a knit hat dallies in the downtown Asheville post office. If you're a police officer, what story are you telling yourself about them? How does the stripe on their pants affect your judgment? Their destination? Their backpack? Skin color?

When Does Lingering Become Malingering?

A man pauses on a street corner. If you live in the area, what do you see? If you're George Zimmerman, the coordinator of a neighborhood watch, you see a suspicious man wearing a hoodie. That might prompt you to call the police or grab your gun and walk out to ask the man his business. If you are Trayvon Martin, it might be your final conversation.

Your Move, Officer

Two people are visiting Pritchard Park. One is sitting at a chessboard, and the other is walking. If you're a police officer, how does motion affect your judgment about which of them might be loitering? Skin color? Chess?

Don't Skulk on the Steps

A man sits on the steps by a fountain at Pritchard Park.

A police officer might accuse him of blocking the steps, a confrontation that might lead to an arrest or worse.

If you were a tourist, would you feel ok about walking by the man? What if he and a friend were sleeping on the steps?

Walking While Black

Is this man loitering? He is WWB (walking while Black) but not blocking shop doors or customers. If you were a police officer, would you talk with him? What if he were walking erratically? Peering into cars? Standing motionless in the lot? What if he were white, wearing a suit, and carrying a briefcase? If it were night, and he was walking through your neighborhood?

Epilogue

What can we do to resist capricious loitering laws—vestiges of Jim Crow—in the United States?

Here are some suggestions from activists:

"Make eye contact and small talk."—Timothy Snyder in *On Tyranny: 20 Lessons from the 20th Century*, 2017. Snyder goes on to write: "This is not just being polite. It is part of being a citizen and a responsible member of society." Do this especially with those we've been conditioned to ignore: panhandlers, the rough-looking, the brown-and-black skinned, those who labor with their hands.

Organize. Pick a local organization that you believe in (your child's school, your church, the school board) and work to make it stronger. Volunteer, run for office. Only well-organized institutions can combat an overreaching government.

Support organizations you believe in. Pick a nonprofit that is doing good work (the ACLU, a food bank) and become a sustaining supporter.

Use your gifts. "We can also think about how we can be most effective, reviewing our personal skill set and talents and the level at which we want to intervene," writes Ruth Ben-Ghiat from *Lucid*. "Are you a community-oriented person? Could you step forth and take a role in your faith, business, sports, or other communities? Can you speak or act effectively at the state level? Have you thought about running for office or working to register people to vote? Are you a facilitator and persuader who can connect with those anchored in the MAGA world?"

Pick one of these 29 "things you can do":

https://www.ifyoucankeepit.org/p/how-you-can-protect-democracy